PLATE 1: *Gerard and Emily.*

PLATE 2: *Emily and Gerard on a beautiful Sunday morning.*

PLATE 3: *Emily and Gerard go to a friend's birthday party.*

PLATE 4: *Gerard has a fencing lesson, while Emily attends her ballet class.*

PLATE 5: *Emily and Gerard are in a school play,* The Princess and the Pirate.

PLATE 6: *Emily has a tea party in her room for her dolls and her stuffed bear.*

PLATE 7: *Gerard has a castle and many toy soldiers in his room.*

PLATE 8: *Emily and Gerard are leaving for a picnic in the woods.*

PLATE 9: *Emily is giving a violin recital this afternoon.*

PLATE 10: *Gerard is flying his kite and playing with his dog Bruno.*

PLATE 11: *Emily and Gerard at the seashore on a fine summer day.*

PLATE 12: *Emily visits Grandmother's farm and feeds the rabbits.*

PLATE 13: *Gerard is a big help to Grandfather on the farm.*

PLATE 14: *Emily enjoys horseback riding on a nice fall day.*

PLATE 15: *Emily and Gerard are going ice skating today.*

PLATE 16: *Emily and Gerard are getting ready for Christmas Day.*